NOVEL PLOTTING

STEP-BY-STEP

2 Manuscripts in 1 Book, Including:
How to Write a Novel and Plotting

Sandy Marsh

Table of Contents

HOW TO WRITE A NOVEL

STEP-BY-STEP

ESSENTIAL ROMANCE NOVEL, MYSTERY NOVEL AND FANTASY NOVEL WRITING TRICKS ANY WRITER CAN LEARN

SANDY MARSH

BOOK 1: HOW TO WRITE A NOVEL

STEP-BY-STEP

Essential Romance Novel, Mystery Novel and Fantasy Novel Writing Tricks Any Writer Can Learn

Sandy Marsh

reparation, damages, or monetary loss due to the information herein, either directly or indirectly.

Respective authors own all copyrights not held by the publisher.

The information herein is offered for informational purposes solely, and is universal as so. The presentation of the information is without contract or any type of guarantee assurance.

The trademarks that are used are without any consent, and the publication of the trademark is without permission or backing by the trademark owner. All trademarks and brands within this book are for clarifying purposes only and are the owned by the owners themselves, not affiliated with this document.

Table of Contents

Introduction

Thank you and congratulations on purchasing *"How to Write a Novel: Step-by-Step | Essential Romance Novel, Mystery Novel and Fantasy Novel Writing Tricks Any Writer Can Learn"*. As well, congratulations on deciding that you want to write a fiction novel!

The tips and tricks you will learn in this book will help walk you through the step-by-step process of writing your very own novel, while also making it extremely easy to stay committed! You will learn everything you need to know about simplifying the process and making it one that you can easily stick to so that you can create the fiction novel of your dreams, literally!

Each chapter in this book is dedicated to one part of the novel writing experience. You will begin by learning all about outlines and work your way through each step right down to finding the perfect reader to test out your new novel. By the time you're done reading this you will be completely finished writing your very own fiction novel.

This book was designed to help make the process easier while also making it an enjoyable experience. Understand that this is not necessarily a "conventional" how-to book as it will seek to both educate and inform while also making the process fun and exciting. Writing a book should never be boring or difficult - if it is, you are going about it all wrong! With the steps in this book, you will learn to bring back the passion in your writing and create the best fiction novel possible, whether this is your first time trying or you've done this before and you just need a boost to get through this particular book!

Please be sure to take your time and have fun with this book as the writing process truly is an experience to be enjoyed. Allow each section to provide you with tips and tricks to help lighten up the experience so that you can increase the entertainment you derive from the writing process so that you are left not only with an incredible novel but also with an experience worth remembering. This book can be used as many times as you require, so be sure to keep it handy for any fiction novels you may set out to write! And lastly, please enjoy!

Chapter 1: The Outline

As you may be aware, having an outline to a book is important. This provides you with an idea of where the story is going and what your "goals" for the book are. Many authors prefer to start with a strong outline that will give them direction and help them stay on track when they are working through the writing process. Having a strong outline that identifies major plot points means that you can continually work your story towards each new plot point in chronological order so that you ultimately end up at your "goal" outcome based on what you had included in your outline.

For many writers, an outline is an absolute must-have. They prefer to have an outline that will help guide them because this keeps them focused and working along a credible storyline that is intended to keep readers engaged. By having this the writer knows how to stay on point and how to structure different parts of the story to keep everything working towards the same goal. For others, having an outline feels too boxy and they feel as though their creative expression is being suffocated by the existence of the outline. If this is you, then you may want to consider scratching the outline altogether. Below we will explore different tips and ideas for each unique individual and how you can create an incredible story regardless of whether or not you choose to use an outline.

If You Love to Guide Your Focus…

If you love to have your focus guided towards a particular goal, such as the one at the end of your outline, then having an outline is a good idea for you. This will help encourage you to stay on track with your writing process and keep each unique element of the story focused towards the outcome. Having the outline helps you avoid yourself from putting unnecessary information in the plot line or otherwise over-explaining things that may not be relevant to the overall story itself.

Outlines are a great tool to help keep writers focused and guided throughout the process. Creating an outline is fairly simple, you think of where you want the characters to "start" and "end" in the story. Then, you decide what major plot points are going to get them from the start to the end. For example, you might have two characters in a romance novel that are going to start as best friends and end as lovers. Along the way, you might choose to include plot points such as them taking on a big project together and it brings them closer, but the competitiveness between them drives them apart. As they work through the competitiveness they discover that their relationship grows even stronger and when they complete the project they are feeling closer than ever before. Later they make excuses to hang out even more, and eventually, they end up falling in love. As you can see from this example, the outline included the main characters, the starting and ending points of the story, and major events that lead the two characters to the "finish line".

Once you have created your basic outline, you want to include even more information in it. This would include settings where each scene takes place, the emotions behind each experience, and anything else that would contribute to you setting the mental image for the scene itself. By identifying as many descriptive factors about each major plot point as possible you make it easier for you to know exactly where you are working towards in each part of the story. Of course, you can always choose to alter these if the writing process brings you towards a different idea or plot point, but having them identified and a rough outline created can help you stay on track and remain focused on what you want to take place within' the story.

If you are someone who tends to need tools such as outlines to help you stay focused and guide you through the process it is a good idea that you complete one before you start writing any part of your novel. Having the outline written and in front of you can help you identify what you like about the story and any issues that you may notice before you actually begin writing. This can help you finalize what your conflict will be an anchor in any specific details that you want to include in your writing so that you go into your novel with a clear plan and an idea of how you are going to achieve what you have set out to accomplish.

If You Love Creative Freedom...

If you are the type of writer who prefers to work alongside creative freedom and who feels suffocated by the idea of having a specific plan to work with there are a few things that you can do in order to exercise your creative freedom while still creating an incredible novel. Just because you don't want to have a specific plan doesn't mean that you cannot create some form of a plan that will help you stay focused and work towards some form of goal throughout your novel.

It is important to understand that even if you prefer having creative freedom, you still need to have some form of outline in place to help you organize your plot and stay focused towards a particular goal. This will help ensure that your book flows in such a way that people will read it and easily work towards the goal with you, rather than attempting to understand why there are so many different pieces of information floating around that seem irrelevant to the book itself.

The first idea you could use is to create a vague outline for your book. This would require you to create an ideal starting point and ending point for your novel, and then fill out the inside of the outline with a few different major plot points that will help guide you from point a to point b. Unlike a complete outline, you will only include enough information to give you a general idea of what you want to include in your book. Then, you can come up with the rest as you are in the process of writing your novel. This can help you with allowing you to have creative expression while also staying focused on the purpose of your novel and working towards it while successfully bringing your reader along with you. Ultimately, it prevents the buildup of irrelevant information or you involving anything that is not necessary to the novel itself.

It will, however, allow you to pick out the details and other smaller factors as you go so that you can allow the story to flow through you naturally, rather than feeling pressured to use extremely specific points in varying areas of your story, potentially taking away from the natural flow that you have created through your creative expression.

Another method you can use is called a hindsight outline. The only two things you need to identify in the beginning of creating this outline is the starting and ending points. You should always have some form of end goal when it comes to writing a novel so that you are clear on what you are writing towards and what you need to be building up to throughout the novel. However, with a hindsight outline, you do not need to include any information beyond these two points. All you have to do is ensure that you are working towards the end goal. As you write major plot points into your story, you can then write them into your outline. This may seem irrelevant, but you will soon understand that writing them down allows you to see where you have come from and where you want to go. It ensures that each part of the plot works together towards the goal and that it makes sense towards the overall story. Doing this prevents you from forgetting about plot points, including ones that may contradict previous ones, and get a general idea of the flow of your story in retrospect, rather than in advance.

Questions to Ask Yourself

The following questions are questions you should ask yourself when you are developing your outline. This will ensure that you have a strong plan for your outline and that no details are missed out on.

1. Where is my protagonist starting?

2. Where are they at in their life in the beginning of the story?

3. Where is my protagonist ending?

4. Where are they at in their life at the end of the story?

5. What major plot points are getting me to (or have gotten me to) the goal?

6. Do these plot points make sense together?

7. Is there anywhere that this outline is weak?

8. What else could I add to my outline to make a rich reading experience?

How you choose to create the outline for your story is unique to you and your writing preferences. Know that you are not required to create a detailed or complete outline before you begin writing your novel. However, having an outline is extremely important as it helps you keep major plot points in chronological order and to ensure that they flow well together. Still, if you prefer to write it out in detail ahead of time, or if you prefer to merely identify your goal and create your outline in hindsight, that is entirely up to you. You should never let creating an outline and identifying specific details of your story hold you back from writing the story in the first place. Knowing that there are options for you to help you stay focused or open up your creative freedom as much as you need to can help ensure that you are not intimidated by the very first step of writing your book. It also helps you feel confident knowing that you can stay focused and still create an incredible book, whether you do it the conventional way or not.

Chapter 2: Your Setting

Developing the setting for your story provides you with the opportunity to have an incredible amount of creative expression. This part of the book is also one of the first times that you will begin to get very descriptive about what is going to happen within' your book. Even if you have a complete outline that is quite detailed, this will be more defined than that.

Your setting is ultimately when and where your story happens. This is something that you need to identify beforehand so that you can keep this information flowing throughout the entire story. For example, you wouldn't want to begin writing a story that was set in the 1800s and then use slang or information that was only relevant to the 2000s or later. Identifying your setting and being very specific and clear on it ensures that your entire book is written with relevance to that setting. The following information will help you identify important tips and tricks that you should pay attention to when it comes to developing your setting for your novel.

If You Only Have One Location

If you are writing a book where the story will never venture away from your primary overall location, then you want to make sure that you are very clear and specific on this location. This is where your entire book is going to be written, so you want to be very descriptive of and clear on this location by knowing exactly what is relevant to it and what is true about it.

You should identify where this location is, what sets it apart from other locations, and why you are using this location. You also want to discover what the local culture is like (specific to your time frame) and any other identifying factors that you may learn about this place. The best way to do it is to research this place as though you were going to be a tourist. Make sure that you do it specific to the time frame, which you will learn more about in a moment. For the location-specific part, however, you want to identify what types of buildings exist in this place, what they were made of, what the roads looked like, what types of wildlife and plant life exists in the area, and anything else that will help you create a graphic image in someone's mind about the location you have chosen.

Once you have identified the location, create a list that involves as many relevant descriptive phrases as you can. You want to generate ideas of how you will describe the place to people throughout the book and creating these ideas beforehand will ensure that you are not at a loss for words or repeating your descriptions throughout the book. Having this list will help you create a dynamic description that truly helps bring the book to life for your readers and prevents them from becoming bored of the same descriptions being used over and over again.

If You Have Many Locations

If you have many locations you want to essentially conduct what you did for one location, only for many. This part of the process may seem fairly straightforward, so we are not going to further explore the process for identifying each unique location. However, there are other things you need to consider when you are using many locations in your book.

First, you want to decide which location is going to be "home" for your characters. This one, in addition to the one where your characters stay in for the longest period of time, should be the ones that you know about the most. You should have plenty of describing factors that help set the scene for what home is like for your characters, as well as for what their new place of residence is like. For example, you might set the scene for home as "The Rocky Mountains: a place where the air is cool and crisp, and the mountainous view is one that cannot be done justice short of seeing it yourself. The community is warm and cozy, especially in the cold winters when snow makes it difficult just to leave your front door." Whereas the new place of residence is described as "The prairies, where the wheat grows for miles and you can see the entire story of the sky as clouds dance across the wide-open view in front of you. The communities are cheerful and bright, and you feel like there is nowhere you can't go, and nothing to stop you from getting where you want to be." You want to describe both the location as previously mentioned and go into detail about the emotion behind each location and why these emotions differ for the protagonist.

Second, you want to identify the mode of travel if any will be used in the book. You also want to become as descriptive as possible when it comes to the mode of transport. Where does the character get on and off of it? What stands out about this mode of transport and how does it contribute to the overall story? Is there anything particular that the reader should know that will help them feel as though they are genuinely walking up to, entering, riding, and exiting the mode of transport that you have chosen? Describing the transport itself in advance will help when it comes to foreshadowing and other story-telling tactics during the writing process. Rather than leaving it up to surprise you can easily blend it into your story so that it flows effortlessly with everything you have already written up until that point, and afterward.

If You Are Making Up the Location

If you are writing a fantasy novel where you are going to be making the location up, it is important that you take the time to actually create a location that makes sense. The location you create needs to be consistent and should be relevant to the story you are telling. There are a few tips when it comes to making up a location that you can consider using to help you create an incredible location for your book.

First, consider basing your location off of somewhere that already exists. If there is somewhere on the globe that resembles what you want your fantasy world to look like, consider first creating a descriptive location setting for that place and then alternating parts of it to fulfill your fantasy world. This will assist you with keeping everything relevant and consistent across your world.

If you are going to be making up the world entirely then you want to take your time. Close your eyes and picture this world in your own mind, first. Then, write as many descriptive factors as you can about the appearance of this location. Ultimately, you want the reader to see exactly what you are seeing in your mind at the time.

You want to make sure that when you are introducing readers to your fantasy world that they feel as though they are mentally stepping into it. They should be able to find enough information in your novel that they can not only step into the world, but they can also interact with it. They should know what type of wildlife - if any - exists in the world. Give them an idea of what the colors are like, how the communities are built, what the buildings themselves look like, and what smells they can find floating around in the air. Give them an idea of what objects are around the setting so that they can mentally picture them and that they truly feel as though they are living in your imaginary world alongside your characters. This will provide you with a strong fantasy setting that will ensure that your book truly is a fantastic read.

If You Only Have One Time Period

When it comes to time periods you need to be very specific and careful. You want to choose one that would make sense to and be relevant to the story you are telling. You also want to ensure that you do enough research about it that you tell the story as though it truly is set in that time frame. A painful mistake that would truly detract from the value of your novel would be one where you choose a certain time frame and then include information that is completely irrelevant to that time frame. For example, if you chose to set your romance novel in the late 1900s but included technology such as cell phones or computers, it would not make sense to the story and would take away from the reading experience.

When you are setting the time frame you want to ensure that you do plenty of research about it. You also want to research your chosen location with relevance to the time frame. What did it look like during that time frame? What was the culture like? What were the people like? How did they treat each other? What was the common slang for that era? You want to be very specific on what it truly would have been like during that time frame so that you can walk your reader through it. Give them the opportunity to feel as though they have stepped into a time portal and they are being transported into that era, whether it be in the present or in the past.

If You Have Many Time Periods

When you are writing a story that has many time periods the tactics you use to develop the setting is similar to if you are writing a story that has many locations. Essentially, you want to ensure that you are effectively researching each time period so that you can provide relevant and factual information based on each time period. You really need to stay focused on the details you are providing so that your reader can easily be walked back and forth with you without finding irrelevant or false pieces of information anywhere within' the text. The more focused and factual you are, the better. When it comes to developing many time periods in a story, there is not much more required than you repeating the research processes several times over for each time period you will write about. Something you may want to add, however, is the mode of transportation being used to transport across time periods. Be sure that you create a piece of machinery and provide enough details about it that you can explain how it works and create a graphic image of it in the minds of your readers.

If You Are Making up the Time Period

If you are making up a time period in your novel, then you need to be extremely descriptive about this time period. You should identify what the time period is, and why it does not already exist. For example, maybe you are generating your own fantasy setting on an alternate planet and Earth has yet to exist therefore the time is not yet in history. Or, perhaps you are writing one in the future and the time has not happened yet, so you are creating it yourself. You need to be able to thoroughly understand *why* you are creating this new time period so that your readers understand as well.

In addition to knowing why, you also need to make up all of the important details about the time period. What is the culture like in this time period? What form of government or authority exists? What do people speak like? Are there any slang words used that your readers may not already know? What do these slang words mean? How do people treat each other? What parts of the community are different from anything we experience in our own world? What else sets this time period apart from what you are presently living or what we already know about? You want to make sure that you go into detail beforehand about creating this time period so that when it comes to the writing process you already know. Doing this will ensure that you stay consistent with your novel and that nothing is added that is then forgotten about and later contradicted. When you are making something up entirely it is important that you put the effort in towards making it truly believable for your readers. This will ensure that they are able to follow the story and that it flows well without having any contradictions, confusing pieces of information, or other additions that otherwise take away from the quality of the story itself.

Combining the Two

The setting of your story is a combination of the time period and the location. When you have completely researched or created each the location and the time period, you must then combine the two. This part of the process is simple, but it is important. You want to make sure that you identify anywhere in the combination where information might contradict itself or take away from the reading experience. For example, if you are writing a book set in the present about an Amish colony that still operates without running water or electricity, you need to identify these factors and explain the discrepancy. Making sure that your time and location mesh together seamlessly and that anything contradictory is explained will ensure that you have a strong setting for your story. This means that you will be able to easily and effortlessly guide your readers through the book without any part of it leading to them wondering what is truly going on with your story.

Questions to Ask Yourself

The following questions are questions you should ask yourself when you are developing your setting. This will ensure that you have a strong plan for your setting and that no details are missed out on.

1. What location(s) will my story take place in?

2. What is unique to this location?

3. How could I describe this location in five sentences or less?

4. When I read that description, can I truly see the location in my mind?

5. Are there any further descriptions I could use to strengthen the visual of my location?

6. What time period(s) will my story take place in?

7. What is unique to this time period?

8. How could I describe this location in five sentences or less?

9. When I read that description, can I truly feel and sense the time period in my mind?

10. Are there any further descriptions I could add to enrich the time period in my story?

11. Do my time period and location make sense together?

12. What describing factors can I use to explain any
discrepancies between my location and time period,
if there are any?

Chapter 3: The Point of View

The next part of writing your story requires you to consider which point of view you want to write from. As an author, you have the opportunity to decide exactly how the reader is going to learn about different elements of your story, as well as how those elements will feel to them. You can do this directly through the use of point of view and which you choose to write your story in.

There are a few different points of view that you can write from when it comes to storytelling. Each one has a unique element that allows you to elaborate on and recall experiences within' the story in a certain way. Some will limit you to only telling it from one perspective whereas others allow you to elaborate with multiple perspectives, or even to provide "outsiders" insight into different experiences. How you choose your point of view will also depend on a few things. Before you choose one, however, let's explore each unique point of view and the advantages and disadvantages it provides you with as a storyteller.

First Person

First person point of view is one of the most popular choices when it comes to writing novels. This is the point of view where the writer refers to the narrator as "I", "we", "me", "mine", "my", and "us". This is similar to if you were telling a story from your own past to someone who was standing in front of you. When you are telling a story from the first-person point of view you must pick which protagonist is going to be the storyteller in your book. Typically, it is the heroic character or the one that is involved in the majority of the scenes that will be chosen as the first-person narrator. However, you can choose virtually anyone you want, dependent upon who is going to be the best angle for you to speak from.

When you write in the first person, you provide a very natural flow to your story. Your reader will feel as though you are telling them *your* story, and if you can effectively captivate them then it will actually begin to feel like your reader is the narrator. Using "I" sentiments and first-person narrative allows your reader to fully immerse themselves in the novel and get a true, deep insight into how the narrator was feeling during each scene. You also only have to pay attention to and fully develop the mind of

one character: the narrators. This is the one that you will need to
have the most insight to. The rest will be based on how the
narrator perceives them, which means that you don't have to go
quite as deep or know every minute detail of each person.
However, this can also lead to some disadvantages. For example,
you are limited to only reflecting on and elaborating the story
based on what the narrator would feel. You cannot explore
anyone else's feelings unless you use tactics such as conversation
to help the narrative character explore the feelings and thoughts
of another. While this is an effective tactic, you aren't going to be
able to use it in every single scene or the story will sound strange
and unnatural. Furthermore, the narrative character must always
be involved in or at the center of every event that takes place in
the book. Otherwise, large portions are going to be missed or you
are going to bounce between different points of view which is not
effective.

Some ways that people have managed to use the first-person
narrative while still maintaining the insights on several characters
at once is by developing books whereby each chapter or section is
narrated by a different character. This provides the reader with
the opportunity to see into several different characters and their
experiences, but it can also jolt the flow of your story and result
in your readers struggling to really connect with each character

the way they could if you maintained a single first-person narrative.

Second Person

Second person is an undesirable choice when it comes to writing fiction, but some people choose to use it when they are writing short stories. This is an interesting point of view to write from, but it rarely creates the ability for an author to produce an entire novel without the novel sounding strange and lacking natural flow. Second person is the "you" narrative, whereby you refer to the person reading or the narrator as "you". For example, "you were standing on a street corner when suddenly someone bumped into you." The entire book would be written in this point of view which, as you might be able to tell, is not ideal. While some books have been written this way, most publishers advise against it and will even refuse to publish books that have been written in this narrative.

The only advantage to writing in the second person narrative is that your book will be unique and eccentric. Based on the nature of this narrative you gain the ability to speak directly to the reader which can be an interesting technique, but it also does not offer you a strong advantage in storytelling. For the most part, anything written in the second person narrative that is longer than a few hundred words feels uncomfortable and sounds "off" to the reader. They will likely grow tired of the eccentric feel and simply begin feeling as though the writing is uncomfortable and strange. Furthermore, it says that you are unprofessional and are inexperienced when it comes to novels. Unless you are a highly experienced writer who has already developed a name for themselves, it is typically best that you avoid this point of view.

Third Person

Third person is the point of view whereby someone completely outside of the story is telling it. For example, using identifiers such as "he" or "she" instead of "I" or "you". This point of view is another popular one when it comes to writing fiction novels because it provides the author with the ability to provide insight into many different elements of each character. It also provides the author with a greater ability to influence the reader's emotions towards various characters without that influence being limited to what would be true and natural for any given character within' the book. For example, perhaps the protagonist hates the antagonist for something he's done wrong. In the first person, you would be required to establish feelings of hatred towards the antagonist. In the third person, however, you can further explain the situation and provide the reader with insight as to how it was a mistake and the protagonist was carrying a grudge over something that was a misunderstanding, for example. It provides you with a stronger power to shape and influence the story in a highly unique way.

When it comes to writing in the third party there are two different types you can write in: third person limited omniscience, or third person unlimited omniscience. Since each one is so unique, we are going to explore them in two different subsections below.

Before we dive in, however, please note that in the following subsections we will discuss a tool many authors use whereby they speak in the third person from a different character's point of view in each scene or chapter. This helps naturally break up the story without confusing the reader along the way. This should not be confused with the technique whereby authors write one chapter per character from the first-person point of view. Although the techniques are virtually the same, they do involve writing from a different point of view in each style.

Third Person Limited Omniscience

Third person limited omniscience means that the author has the power to enter the mind of only a few characters within' the novel. Usually, during this type of experience, the author would write from the point of view of one character per chapter or per scene to avoid confusion. When it comes to this viewpoint, the author would still write with the "he" or "she" descriptors, but would primarily focus on one character per scene or chapter.

This point of view provides the author with the opportunity to enrich the experience by providing viewpoints from many different characters, thereby giving the reader a greater amount of detail and depth into each scene and experience within' the book. It also provides the author the opportunity to write from a broader scope where they are not required to limit their story to a single person's experiences. Instead, you can elaborate on experiences that may take place without one or more of the character's present. The biggest disadvantage of this is that for the author it requires you to take more time to make each part of the book flow naturally, as well as to provide distinctive voices for each character so as not to confuse yourself or your reader. Furthermore, if you switch too often you will break up the flow of your story and create an unnatural and uncomfortable. It is important that you take your time and truly dedicate if you are going to use this practice, also. Many authors find that they write in this point of view for a few chapters and then they wind up writing from the first-person narrative for the remainder of the book. This laziness can result in your first chapters, or last chapters needing to be repaired so that the entire book is written in the same narrative and flows smoothly.

Third Person Unlimited Omniscience

Third person, unlimited omniscience is virtually the same as limited omniscience, except that the author is not restricted to only sharing the experience from a few character's points of view. Instead, they can shift into the mind of any character within' the story and provide their viewpoint on the events that are taking place.

While this may provide the author with the opportunity to elaborate and provide great detail and depth to the story, it can also result in them getting far too carried away if they are not careful. Writing from too many different points of view can diffuse the entire story and result in the author washing out any storyline that may have taken place. It is similar to the mistake of oversharing or otherwise providing far too much information, well beyond what the reader needs to know. Although it may give them a strong understanding of each scene, it can also cause for it to take far too long to "get to the point already". It is generally advised against the idea of you writing in third person unlimited omniscience unless you are using the technique strategically to avoid damaging your storyline.

How to Choose

There is one incredibly each tactic to use when it comes to deciding which point of view you want to use when it comes to sharing your story. Consider taking one small scene from the book and then writing that scene in three different narratives: first person, third person limited omniscience, and third person unlimited omniscience. Only write a few short paragraphs in each point of view so that it doesn't take too long, but be sure that you write them well. Then, read each one. This will give you an idea as to how each point of view would shape the reader's experience and what "feel" it gives to your story. It also provides you with some practice as to how each point of view feels as the author and if it gives you the ability to express yourself in the way that you want to be expressed.

Questions to Ask Yourself

The following questions are questions you should ask yourself when you are choosing your point of view. This will ensure that you have a strong plan for your point of view and that no details are missed out on.

1. Who do I want to tell my story?

2. What feeling do I want my readers to have?

3. Which point of view is going to be reasonable for me to write an entire novel in?

4. Will this give me the opportunity to express my story the way I want to?

5. Is there any way that this might limit my story or otherwise hinder the reader's experience?

Chapter 4: Characters

Naturally, your story needs characters. After all, what story are you telling if there is no one taking part in the story itself? Creating a strong story requires for you to have strong, well-developed characters involved. If you are looking for greater insight as to how you can develop well-rounded characters I encourage you to read book 6 from this series: "*Character Development*: Step-by-Step." Because I provide you with such great detail on how to develop your characters in that novel, I will not go into elaborate detail on character development in this chapter. Instead, we are going to identify other important information about your characters, such as who needs to be involved in the story and how they contribute. Knowing this basic information is powerful in regard to the actual writing process. This will help you when it comes to outlining and creating a plan for the direction of your story. When it comes to the actual writing process, however, you will want to make sure that you have fully developed characters so that they are realistic and can add to your story in a powerful way. In the meantime, let's explore other important aspects of characters in your story.

The Value of Your Characters

Characters are a powerful element of your story because they truly drive the story forward. Without characters, the story simply cannot move forward because there would be nothing to talk about. Your characters help you not only convey the story but also express it in certain ways. Depending on what point of view you have chosen, your characters can be used in unique ways to manipulate the reader's thoughts and feelings about other characters, as well as about the storyline and events that take place within' the story.

Think of professional dancers. Music is put on as the foundation for the story and it can be related to the setting. The words that coincide with the music, or the song lyrics, are responsible for providing you with insight into what the song is about. Once the dancers begin dancing, however, they can manipulate how you feel about the song, what emotions are provoked within' you, and how you take in the experience as a whole. Without the dancers, it would simply be a song with lyrics. With the dancers, it is a story with a soul.

The same goes with writing books. The setting is the foundation for your story, and the narrator is the one who tells the story. Your characters, however, provide the heart and soul of your story. They are the ones that you can use to help manipulate the readers' thoughts and provoke different emotions in them so that they experience the book in the way that you want them to. While each unique reader may have a slightly different experience, the overall interpretation of the book will remain fairly similar if you use your tools or characters, properly.

Choosing Your Protagonist

Because of how important characters are, it is vital that you choose a good character to be your protagonist. Your protagonist needs to be a strong character who can lead the story in a powerful way. When you are putting together the outline and idea for your story, consider which specific character would be best at bringing readers through the story in an effective manner that would allow you to create the experience you want to create. Which of your characters will be involved in the most experiences? Which ones will have the best emotional attachment to the storyline so that they can move your readers for you? If you are writing from a first-person narrative, you need to choose a single character that is going to be able to effectively move everyone through the entire novel. For example, it may be the wife, best friend, teacher, and book club host. Because this particular character is involved in so many different elements of the community she may be the best individual and voice to help you tell the story with a great level of depth and dynamic so that the reader truly has an incredible experience. If you are writing in the third party, however, make sure that you choose powerful characters that you will write from. These would-be ones that all connect in one way or another and that have stories that will link together. This ensures that each character makes sense to the narrative. If you are writing in third-party unlimited omniscience, make sure that when you move to the narrative of someone who may be new or unique to a specific part of the story that this move makes sense and it is clear to the reader as to why you are doing this. This will ensure that you are drawing the reader through a clear and logical storyline that makes sense.

How Many Characters Do You Really Need?

The number of characters you choose to have in your story is really unique to the story you are trying to tell. If you are telling a romance novel, for example, you may only have two primary characters and a handful of other characters that contribute to the story. For example, some best friends, family members, the cashier at the drug store they always stop at, or the receptionist at the hotel where they celebrate their honeymoon. When you are planning your story, you need to consider how many characters are actually going to be required in order for you to tell the story. As you carry on you may discover that you need to add more characters along the way, so it is not mandatory for you to identify every single character you are going to write about immediately. However, you should have a good idea of who your primary and secondary characters are going to be. Remember, your primary characters are the ones that show up in nearly all scenes and your secondary ones are characters that are recurring in a major way.

What Your Characters Say About Your Book

The characters you choose are going to say a lot about the book you are writing and the story you are telling. These characters have the power to shape the reader's perception of the book, as well as gain an even deeper insight as to what the setting is like and the feelings they should be deriving from the general information you are providing. For example, if you are writing a book from the late 1990's about a town in the southern states, you could write about a wealthy family or a poor family. This would shape your character's point of view on the entire setting and emotions associated with the book, as well as how they perceive your characters. It also helps round out your story. The characters you choose, how you design them, and how you portray them will all contribute to the story you tell. In the previous example, one story might provide the reader with a country glamorous feeling where they ride horses and own a large farm with stable hands, whereas the other might provide your family with a poorer country feel where they *are* the stable hands and they live in a shack built on the corner of the property. Who you choose for your characters will provide greater depth for your story and ultimately be the final factor that provides your reader with the clear picture of what they see, think, and feel as they read the story you have written for them.

Questions to Ask Yourself

The following questions are questions you should ask yourself when you are developing the basic outline for your characters. This will ensure that you have a strong plan for your character development and that no details are missed out on. Remember to check out book 6 where we go deeper into the creation and development of characters so that you have a strong selection of characters to help move your story forward.

1. What story am I telling and who is the focus of the story?

2. What point of view am I writing in and whose point of view do I want to write from?

3. What recurring characters are an important element of this story?

4. Are there any additional characters that will be involved in key plot points?

5. How do these specific characters help move the story?

Chapter 5: Conflict

Every good novel comes with a fair amount of conflict involved. If there was no conflict, then there would be nothing that really keeps the reader engaged. Everyone loves a great happy-ending story, but most like to see the work that goes into creating that happy ending. This is somewhat like providing a realistic snippet of your character's lives to your readers. No one's real life is easy all of the time, so writing an entire novel where all of your characters never experience any true conflict is not only unrealistic but also boring. It takes away from the entire reading experience by never giving any depth or diversity to your story.

Creating conflict in your novel should be an ongoing process. It is not simply about having one major conflict and everything being sunshine and rainbows up until and after that point. Instead, it is about leading up to the conflict, and about coming down from it as well. You want to have one primary conflict that drives the story, but you should include many other conflicts along the way as well. These smaller conflicts add more depth and reality to your story, but they also help you lead your reader through many triumphs and victories with the characters. Each time your character overcomes something your reader will feel as though they overcame it together and it will bond the reader to your character even more. Furthermore, it stops you from writing an unrealistic story that goes from bad to much worse and then suddenly great again. It provides you with a natural and lifelike flow that allows your reader to feel as though they are genuinely connecting with an individual and not a character that you have made up for the purpose of writing a novel.

Types of Conflict

There are a couple of different types of conflict that exist in every novel. The first one is considered a primary conflict. This is the primary purpose of why you are telling the story, and it is what you will lead up to and wind down from throughout the process of writing the novel. This is the "big one" that will keep your readers engaged and have them feeling like they *need* to know what happens after that particular conflict takes place.

The next type is secondary conflict. This is the type of conflict that takes place leading up to and after the primary conflict. These are smaller conflicts that exist in addition to the primary conflict. For example, maybe in an action-based novel the kidnapper is about to drive a car off of a bridge, so the protagonist has to go save the person who has been kidnapped, but they can't do that until they can get a car because the kidnapper has their car. Here, the kidnapper driving off the bridge would be the primary conflict and the lack of a car would be the secondary conflict. In the grand scheme of the entire story, however, both would be secondary to the greater problem which is that someone has been kidnapped. When you build on the conflict in this way it diversifies everything and adds a more realistic and compelling story base that drives readers forward. Now, they want to know where the protagonist gets the car from if they reach the kidnapper on time, and how they save the person who has been kidnapped. As you can see, it would keep them engaged.

The third type of conflict is an alternate conflict. In a story where third person point of view is used, the author may choose to have two or three primary conflicts going on. For example, for the parents getting divorced might be the primary conflict, for one kid her social life falling apart might be the primary conflict, and for the second kid choosing which parent to live with might be the primary conflict. This story would run with each of these conflicts equally as important as the other, and each one drives part of the story forward until it all reaches an ending whereby everyone is satisfied and happy with the outcome.

When the Conflict Should Occur

Choosing when the conflict should occur in your book is important. There are many different points at which you might desire to put the primary conflict into your plotline. However, it is imperative that you give your reader a reason to care by infusing some form of conflict into the first ten pages.

Some authors choose to start out within' the first ten pages by introducing the primary conflict and then providing the remainder of the wind-down story from there. For example, elaborating further on the plotline where someone is kidnapped, you may write that said person was kidnapped on the first page, or within' the first ten pages. The rest of the book would then be a series of secondary conflicts that result from the primary conflict, until the end where the person is rescued.

Other authors do not want to reveal the primary conflict right away and choose to save it for later. Some prefer to put it somewhere in the middle of the book and provide a fairly even amount of writing leading up to the conflict and winding down from it, whereas others like to put it towards the end of the story and use the winding down process as the opportunity to introduce the "happily ever after" experience.

Where you prefer to put the conflict in your own story heavily depends on how quickly you want your readers to move through the conflict, as well as how you want the conflict to leverage the story overall. If you want it to be the primary focus of the story, you may want to introduce it sooner or at least use secondary conflicts to suggest it starting right away. However, if you want the happily-ever-after story to be the primary focus of the story then you may want to use more casual secondary conflicts to keep the reader engaged while building them up to the conflict and then using the resolution as your final happily-ever-after scene.

Regardless of how you choose to infuse the story with your conflict, one thing remains consistent: you need to give the reader a reason to continue reading your book. Within' the first ten pages your reader needs to understand why they should fall in love with the book through developing relationships with the characters, understanding the importance of the conflicts and how they affect the characters, and what they can expect to feel when reading the book. All of this can be done by how you introduce the conflict, and when.

Questions to Ask Yourself

The following questions are questions you should ask yourself when you are developing your conflict. These questions will ensure that you are clear on what your conflict is and how it affects the story you are telling.

1. What is the primary conflict taking place in my novel?

2. How many primary conflicts do I want involved in my novel? (Note: if you are telling a story from the first person, choose one or two at most.)

3. What type of secondary conflicts can I use to build up to the primary conflict?

4. What secondary conflicts would work well to help me wind down from the conflict?

5. How do I want the conflict to drive my novel forward?

6. When do I want to introduce the conflict and how will that affect the reading experience?

7. Does the conflict make sense to the novel?

8. Does the conflict provide enough reason for the reader to truly care?

9. If I am not introducing my primary conflict right away, what conflict can I use to compel my reader to continue reading?

Chapter 6: Additional Tips

In addition to the basics of writing your novel, there are many additional tips that you can use when it comes to generating a high-quality fiction-based novel that will not only impress yourself but your audience as well. Using these tips when you are writing your story will help you increase the joy you get from the process while also increasing the value of your work. These tips are selected from a series of professional writers and have helped them in the process of generating their own fiction novels. Remember, however, not everyone is the same and therefore you may not require all of these tips when it comes to writing your own novel. Take what feels right for you and your unique story and leave the rest!

As mentioned in the introduction of this book, the tips and information provided within' this book is unique and issued to help you not only create higher quality materials but also enjoy the process. Writing your novel should be an experience that you gain joy from, not one that stresses you out or makes you feel incompetent. If you are struggling, you are not doing it right. The following tips can help take you out of the struggling mode and put you back in the mood to enjoy the experience. When the process is light and enjoyable you will likely find that you produce much better work, so be sure to slow down and readdress your approach if you are struggling to produce the results you desire.

Finally, because of the fact that some of these tips may not apply to the unique book you are writing, you will likely want to keep this information handy for any additional projects you may desire to accomplish. Some of these tips may be more relevant to certain types of books than they are to others, therefore you are likely to find value in new and unique ways each time you return to this book.

Think Outside of the Box

When it comes to writing stories, there are many plotlines that exist that are simply rewritten with different angles and different characters. The setting may be different and some of the events that take place may alter, but ultimately the entire story works out to be similar to several other books within' the same genre. Although the saying "don't try to reinvent the wheel" may ring true in many cases, it is not always the best approach to take when you are attempting to write a new and interesting book that will engage your readers in a powerful way.

Instead of trying to recreate a tired plotline, try thinking outside of the box entirely. Consider the genre you are writing for, such as romance, mystery, or fantasy, and spend some time thinking about parts of the story that are never typically told within' traditional novels from that genre. As you discover new parts of the story that you can emphasize on, make sure that you are truly criticizing them to ensure that there is a good reason as to why this part of the story hasn't been told before. Sometimes a certain element may be rejected or ignored because there simply isn't enough to talk about, other times it may be because that isn't the traditional approach, therefore, most people don't consider it when they are writing a novel in that genre.

Looking at things from a different perspective and discovering new ways to share a story provides your book with a unique twist that allows you to engage your readers not only through incredible work but also through the element of surprise. For example, most romance novels lead up to the part where the lovers fall in love, but what if your novel was more focused on the wind-down? What if the marriage happened within' the first ten pages and from there it was the wind-down and told the next part of the romance story that most novels don't focus on? Paying attention to unique elements of the story gives you the opportunity to still write in your chosen genre while also having the chance to put a unique spin on things and create a story that people weren't expecting.

Ditch Expectations

When it comes to the writing world you will likely stumble on expectations from many different people. Publishers, readers, yourself, other authors, everyone has an expectation of what a book "should" be like. While it is important to consider these elements, especially since some of them can make or break the success of your book, it is also important to ditch the pressure that comes along with them.

Most writers can agree that feeling too much pressure can result in writer's block and it can also drown the enjoyment you gain from writing the book. It can make it feel too much like work and less like an experience to be enjoyed by both you and the readers. Instead of putting that much pressure on yourself, ditch expectations and write for the trashcan. You will likely be surprised at the quality of work you produce when you aren't considering all of the technical aspects of your book.

Set Deadlines

Having deadlines set in place can help you keep motivated, and it can also help you plan for other parts of the book writing process. For example, this can help you decide when you need to begin approaching publishers when work needs to be handed in, when marketing efforts should commence, and more. Having deadlines in place keeps everything moving forward and prevents you from avoiding or neglecting your book altogether.

When you are setting deadlines, however, be generous with yourself. Do not set a deadline that is fixed on a date that requires you to work an obscene amount each day from where you are now until the deadline arrives. Doing this will bring back the pressure and take away the joy of the writing experience. Instead of writing and allowing the story to flow through you, you will be writing under the pressure of knowing that if you don't get a certain amount of words out *right now* that you will officially be late for your deadline and everything will be hindered by your lack of writing speed. Instead, choose a generous deadline that gives you plenty of time to take breaks, step aside and get a breather, and come back to your work to finish it. Be kind to yourself and account for breaks. Most writers do not write an entire book in one straight shot. Instead, they write for several days, or even weeks, and then take breaks off in between to allow for more inspiration to come to them before they carry on. Give yourself the opportunity to have these breaks so that you can take them without feeling pressure.

Get a Good "Test" Reader

When your book is complete, you need to have a good test reader who can read through it for you. This is someone who is not necessarily looking for grammatical errors or otherwise editing your book. Rather, they are simply reading to see if it is engaging and if it will actually appeal to your audience. Naturally, this person should identify with your target audience or their opinion may not count for much.

It is important that you do not hand your book to everyone you know and get as many people as possible. Instead, pick one or *maybe* two test readers who identify with your target audience and allow them to read the book. This way you can get honest opinions without feeling overwhelmed by a number of responses you get. It also helps open your purchasing audience because your friends and family will likely be some of your earliest buyers once your title is launched.

Avoid Perfectionism

Many writers put a pressure on themselves to create the perfect piece of work. They may think of an artist they already know or a series of books they have read that they perceive as perfect and they want their books to be the same quality. Understand that this is not valuable to the writing process and it can actually hold you back from producing high-quality work.

Perfectionism can be intimidating, and it can have you overly critical of the work you are producing. Most of the best books that exist on shelves today were not subjected to perfectionism. Instead, the author focused on telling a great story, not a perfect one. Readers are not expecting a perfect book, they are expecting one that takes them through the story in such a way that is engaging and makes them genuinely feel as though they are present and can relate to what they are reading. Perfectionists need not worry.

Write What You Don't Know

There is a long-standing piece of advice that tells writers to "write what they know", but this isn't always the best way to go. Unless you are deeply passionate about your topic and can infuse it with all of the emotions related to that passion, consider writing what you *don't* know.

Think about a topic that interests you and things you would have to learn based on that new interest. Then, spend time researching it for the purpose of writing the book. For example, if your protagonist is a karate star, consider going to a few karate lessons to get a first-hand idea of what it is like so that you can write from within' the experience. Writing in this way gives you a better opportunity to convey the excitement that you are feeling through your story, thus translating it into the reader's experience.

When we write about what we know, we often don't have the same level of excitement or passion as we would if we were brand new to the knowledge because we have a "been there, done that" feeling towards the topic. Even when we are passionate about it, it can be hard to convey that new childlike wonder through the story. When you are brand new, however, it is brand new to you *and* the reader, and it can enhance the quality of your story through all of the exciting emotions you infuse it with.

Manipulate Your Reader's Emotions

Readers are most often attracted to books that draw out a variety of emotions in them. You want to use your characters and the storyline to manipulate your reader's emotions so that they are emotionally drawn to and attached to the book as you are reading. Many readers agree that the best books are the ones that leave you with a "lost" feeling when you put them down. This is because the reader has developed an emotional attachment to the book, likely based on the writer's technique.

You can manipulate your reader's emotions through a variety of different plot points, experiences, and descriptive phrases. You want to start by helping them become emotionally connected to one or more of the characters, then subject these characters to various experiences that draw out certain emotions in the characters. As a result, it will draw out emotions in your readers as well.

When your reader is emotionally connected to the book, they are far more engaged and much more likely to read it all the way through. Furthermore, they are much more likely to genuinely enjoy the book. Make sure that you play with several different emotions so that the book is not excessively sad, angry, funny, or otherwise. Even if you want to emphasize on one emotion more than the rest, be sure to add a healthy mixture of other emotions so that the book does not become predictable or boring.

Conclusion

Thank you for reading *"How to Write a Novel: Step by Step | Essential Romance Novel, Mystery Novel and Fantasy Novel Writing Tricks Any Writer Can Learn"*!

I hope that this book was able to provide you with many tips and tricks to assist you in the process of writing your very own fiction novel. Whether you are writing a romance novel, a mystery novel, or a fantasy novel, I hope that you were able to learn many valuable methods to increase the enjoyment of the experience and increase the quality of your work overall. This book was designed to help you master the writing process, and I hope that you were able to learn plenty of new and diverse information in order to help you do so.

The next step is to start writing! If you haven't already, begin with your outline and move forward from there. As you are working on your book, be sure to check back with this guidebook regularly to see if there are any tips or tricks related to the part of the process you are presently in. This book was written to be a writing resource that you can check back to as often as you need, so don't hesitate to keep it handy during the entire writing process. You never know what part of the book might become valuable to you during each unique part of the process!

Thank you, and enjoy!

PLOTTING

STEP-BY-STEP

ESSENTIAL STORY PLOTTING, CONFLICT WRITING AND PLOTLINE TRICKS ANY WRITER CAN LEARN

SANDY MARSH

BOOK 2: PLOTTING

STEP-BY-STEP

Essential Story Plotting, Conflict Writing and Plotline Tricks Any Writer Can Learn

Sandy Marsh

reparation, damages, or monetary loss due to the information herein, either directly or indirectly.

Respective authors own all copyrights not held by the publisher.

The information herein is offered for informational purposes solely and is universal as so. The presentation of the information is without a contract or any type of guarantee assurance.

The trademarks that are used are without any consent, and the publication of the trademark is without permission or backing by the trademark owner. All trademarks and brands within this book are for clarifying purposes only and are the owned by the owners themselves, not affiliated with this document.

Table of Contents

Conclusion **131**

Introduction

Thank you and congratulations for purchasing *"Plotting: Step-by-Step | Essential Story Plotting, Conflict Writing and Plotline Tricks Any Writer Can Learn"*.

In this book, we are going to further explore how you can write a rich plot that will not only give you plenty of material to write about but will also give you a depth of material that takes your story to the next level. The goal of designing a plotline is to establish a rich story that will intrigue your readers and give you, as the writer, the opportunity to have maximum impact on your storytelling process. Through creating a strong and productive plotline, you give yourself the power to take your story to greater heights and leave your readers with more to take away from the story itself in terms of lessons, experience, and entertainment.

Throughout this book, you are going to learn more about how you can write your own plot in such a way that will help you achieve those next-level results. You will learn about the basic structure of a plotline, as well as how you can build your own plot around this structure. Then, you will be guided through the process of taking your plot outline and bringing it to life in such a way that enables you to use this plotline for maximum impact. Finally, you will learn about some tips and tricks straight from the pros of story writing themselves. In this final chapter, you will be provided with everything you need to tie up any loose ends and make sure that you have a rock solid plotline that will drive your story forward in the most powerful, rewarding, and non-expecting ways possible.

If you are ready to learn how you can create the best plotline ever, and how you can execute it in your writing process so that it has maximum impact, then you are in the right place. Please take your time and build your plot alongside this book so that you can take in every piece of advice being offered and apply it to your own plot building practice. This will ensure that you are benefiting from all of the knowledge within' this book and that you have the best possible results. And of course, enjoy!

Chapter 1: A Basic Plot Outline

Plot outlines, like with story outlines and story structures, have a specific sequence that they are usually created in. While you can choose to alter the timing of this sequence, it is always best that you stick to the sequence itself. This will ensure that you are using the proper and best outline available to help you create a rich and powerful plot. In this chapter, you are going to explore what this basic outline is, as well as every element that exists in this outline. You will also gain an understanding as to why the structure is built this way, and how this contributes to your successful story plot. By the end, you should have a strong understanding as to how this structure works, why it works, and how it looks in stories when it has been executed effectively.

What is the Purpose of The Plot Outline?

Like with all of the elements of your story that we have discussed until now, the plot outline or plot diagram has a very profound and powerful purpose when it comes to your story writing process and experience. This tool is specifically used to help you choose major plot points and organize them along a story arc so that you can identify what your story will be like beforehand. The reason you do this is for several reasons, though it is primarily for the purpose of organizing your plot sequencing so that the story pans out in a strong, chronological manner that allows it to flow efficiently and effectively.

Many people believe that using something such as a plot outline will restrict the writing process and prevent them from having creative freedom and expression when it comes to writing the novel. There are many ways to help further open up the opportunity for creative expression, but ultimately this is not the case. Having a plot outline does not need to mean that you specifically plan out each minor element of your book before you get to the writing process. Instead, it gives you the opportunity to get an overall idea of where you are going with your novel and how you can get there while providing and delivering the best story possible. This is more about embracing your creative freedom and using it to guide you towards a story that leaves a massive impact on your readers than it is about eliminating your creative freedom and forcing you to think about all of the details *right now* rather than as they come to you.

Plot outlines serve as a great backbone to your story. These provide the bare bone basics of your story, what you want to include in it, and how you want to deliver it to your readers. As you are writing, you still have the power to switch things around, including enormous amounts of creativity in the actual writing process, and otherwise, add your own personal touch to your novel. Having the plot outline simply means that you know what general direction to head in and when and where things should happen within' your book so that you are capable of delivering a strong story that has the ability to engage, impress, and excite your readers, no matter what genre you are writing in.

What the Outline Looks Like

The outline looks somewhat like an unfinished triangle or the moving chart that gathers information on a person's heartbeat.

It starts out as a flat line, spikes up to create a triangular shape, and then comes back down to the flat line. This is the most basic plot outline that exists, and it is the one that virtually every story follows. Although you may slightly alter where the spike exists on your own diagram, or how much rising action and falling action exist before and after the spike, the shape remains generally untouched, and it serves as an excellent representation of what your plot outline should look like. Because of the shape of this spike, it is also known as a story arc.

Where the plotline starts, with the flatline, is known as an exposition. This is the beginning of your novel, and it serves by providing you with the opportunity to introduce your characters and the other important elements of the book. This is where you want to introduce the setting of your novel, the stakes that your character(s) are concerned about, and what the problem is. It is through this that you gain the momentum within your novel that will allow you to accelerate towards the problem while keeping your reader engaged, as here is where you give them a reason to care and have the interest to keep reading what you have written.

Once you have successfully completed the exposition, you want to introduce the rising action. This is the part of the story where you practice suspense-building techniques to keep your reader engaged and involved. You are using this part of the book to climb towards the climax of the story. Here, the problem that your character(s) are facing is getting worse, and the complications are exceeding. Usually, this rising action takes course over many pages and even chapters so that you can generate a large element of suspense before you eventually arrive at the climax. Here, you can introduce problems and solve them all well before reaching the actual climax. The primary purpose is to draw the story up to where "it" happens, with "it" being the big reason why you are telling the story in the first place.

The climax is usually around the middle of the story, though it can take place sooner or later depending on how you have chosen to write the story and where you have introduced each unique plot element. This is the most exciting and typically most rewarding part of the story, especially for readers, because it gives them satisfaction after all of the rising action you have shared with them until now. This is the part that makes the reader question "what's next?" and want to keep reading to find out.

Once you have worked through the climax of your story, you officially fall into a decline otherwise known as falling action. This is where the "what now?" part of the climax is revealed as you give your reader an idea of what the resolution is following the climax of your story. You use this as an opportunity to tie up loose ends, to explain where things go after the climax, and to give your reader an opportunity to reflect on the rest of the story. You answer any questions that may have been left behind throughout the rest of the story and generally work towards closing *most* things off in this area. This is where you are working towards the resolution.

The end of the story is also known as the resolution, and this is where the resolution is actually identified. You use this part of the book to inform your reader as to how the resolution has affected each character, how things have turned out for them, and where they are now that the story's problem has been resolved. You close up all of the final loose ends here and provide answers to any unanswered questions. This is where you ultimately provide closure for your book, your characters, and your reader.

Following this plot outline or diagram gives you the opportunity to use a story arc that works. Virtually every story is built along this diagram in one way or another. Sometimes the climax takes place sooner or later than the center of the story, but this is typically how books are written. This outline is used because it works, but also because it gives you a structured outline to help you write the information that your readers need in order for the story to have a positive impact on them. Using this story arc or plot diagram gives you the opportunity to have plenty of time to introduce different elements of the story and explain them in enough detail that your reader has time to collect all of the information they need to experience the story in a powerful manner.

Examples of Plot Outlines

There are many examples of plot outlines available to you, especially if you are an avid reader, television or movie watcher, or story listener. Virtually every story you have ever heard follows this structure in one way or another. However, to give you a few easy ideas of how this outline looks when it is in practice, let's look at two unique stories: The Three Little Pigs and Cinderella.

In three little pigs, we are introduced through the exposition where the three pigs are moving away from their family home, and each is in search of a new home. We are presented with who they are, what they are doing, and why. We are also given an idea of what is at stake for them: their homes. It moves forward into the rising action when we learn about each of the pigs looking for building materials and then building their homes. We learn that one builds theirs out of a weaker material (straw), one builds theirs out of a stronger material (twigs), and one builds theirs out of the strongest material (bricks). We are informed about the varying strengths of these materials, giving us the idea that there is some importance behind this piece of information but not yet introducing why. The story continues to rise as we later are introduced to the big bad wolf who comes along and huffs and puffs to blow down the first house which is made of straw. As you likely already know, the house blows down right away, and the pig runs off to his brother's house, which is made of twigs. The big bad wolf then goes and blows down the twig house and huffs and puffs and blows down that house as well. So, the two pigs are left running away to their other brother's house, which is made of bricks. There, the pigs are safe from the big bad wolf's huffing and puffing. The climax of the story arrives when the wolf finds a way to climb onto the roof of the house and comes down the chimney. There, he falls into a pot of boiling water, and the pigs cook him up. The falling action is that the pigs enjoy a feast together and are free of their fear of being eaten up by the big bad wolf. The resolution is that the three pigs end up sharing the home together and living with each other "happily ever after."

Cinderella is another popular fairy tale which also introduces us to what a plot diagram looks like in action. Here, the exposition lies within' Cinderella being introduced to the readers. We learn that she is a step-child and that her dad is no longer around, so she lives with her evil step-mom and two evil step-sisters. The step-mom and step-sisters live selfish lives of happiness and joy whilst forcing Cinderella to take care of the household by overseeing the chores and ensuring that it is well looked after. The rising action is when Cinderella overhears about an upcoming ball and insists that she wants to go. The step-mom says she can only go if all of her work is complete, and then ensures that there is so much work to be done that Cinderella will never be done in time. A fairy godmother comes and grants Cinderella her wish of going to the ball. She even ensures that Cinderella has a beautiful outfit and that she is cleaned up nicely for the experience so that she isn't late and all she has to do is get there. The climax arrives when Cinderella is at the ball. There, the prince falls in love with her and insists that they get married. When she realizes that the clock is about to strike midnight, she runs out without leaving her name or any contact information with the prince. However, she does lose a glass slipper on her way out of the ball. The falling action starts when the prince picks up the shoe and insists that he and his servants find Cinderella. They take the glass slipper and visit every house in the land to find the lady whom the glass slipper belongs to. Cinderella is almost robbed of the opportunity to try on the glass slipper when her step-mother tries to lock her in the basement, but she manages to get out. The resolution is finally granted to us when we learn that the glass slipper fits her perfectly and she is, in fact, the lady that the prince wanted to marry the night before. The step-mom is furious and so are the step-sisters as they learn that they are not the one who gets to marry the prince. Cinderella, on the other hand, is granted the opportunity to marry the prince, and she is freed from her life as a servant for her ungrateful and evil step-mom and step-sisters.

As you can see in both of these stories, there are very clear expositions, rising actions, climaxes, falling actions, and resolutions. These are the primary requirements of a story to keep it moving so that readers remain engaged and curious about how the story ends. Without these primary elements, the story may become stagnant, fail to draw readers through a chronological series of events that flow effectively through the storyline or otherwise deliver the story in such a way that helps us stay invested in it and curious as to what the resolution will be. Ultimately, the entire purpose of these plot diagrams is to ensure that your reader stays engaged with what the outcome will be, as you can see with these two examples.

Chapter 2: Building Your Plot

Now that you are aware of how a plot should look, it is time to begin building your own! In this chapter, we are going to explore the various steps of building your own plot line. You will be given all of the information you need to move from start to finish effectively. Even if you are not already aware of what your story is going to be, you will be given the opportunity to generate an idea within' this chapter. This chapter is all about helping you come up with a great idea and transform it into a powerful plot line that will help you generate a moving and engaging story that keeps your readers invested until the very end.

Step One: Get Inspired

The first part of writing a plot for your story is to get inspired. If you haven't already got an idea of what you want your story to be about, look for inspiration to help you pick a topic. You can find inspiration for stories in all areas of life from your day-to-day life to stories that other people tell you. You may even be able to reflect back on certain parts of your life or the life of someone you know and draw on experiences to help you become inspired on what you should write your book about. Alternatively, you may draw inspiration from other stories that you have heard or read. Ensure that when you are picking your story, however, that you don't directly copy someone else's story as this is a form of plagiarism. If you are drawing on inspiration from a story you've already heard or read before, take the time to look at the story from unique angles to see how you could write the same story only from a completely different perspective, potentially even with a different outcome altogether.

If you already have an idea of what you want to write your story about, take the time now to elaborate on that idea in your head. Look at it from all angles and see how you can ensure that you have a rich topic that will provide you with the opportunity to draw on it for plenty of material and substance to build your story from. You want to make sure that you have the entire idea of the story beforehand so that you have a general idea of where to go during the writing process. While you can certainly go ahead without a general idea, you will be losing all purposes of writing a plot line. And, ultimately, you will end up writing a story with no sense of direction that may result in you having a very bland, unexciting and otherwise boring story.

Step Two: Getting Direction

Now that you have generated your idea for what you want to write about, it is time to give yourself a sense of direction. This will ensure that you are clear on the focus of your story so that you can remain focused during the writing process. Creating a sense of direction for your story is extremely simple. Once you have generated the entire idea of what you want your story to be about, simply sum it all up into one sentence. Being able to sum it up in a single sentence means that you have clarity on what your story is and you are also clear on what the outcome will be. The outcome is ultimately what you need to know to have a sense of direction as this is what you are going to be writing toward. Below are a few examples of sentences that identify the entire plot of a story in a few words.

"An estranged sister returns to her brother's life so she can take his money and buy her way out of a dangerous situation."

"A bartender falls deeper in love with a regular patron each time he visits her bar and eventually they fall in love, get married, and buy the bar."

"A surgeon who is murdered by his patient that is a victim of neurotic episodes was believed to be a tragic victim, but later they discover that he was actually holding some very sensitive information that ultimately got him killed."

As you can see, each of these sentences gives a very direct insight as to what the story is going to be about and who is involved. It shows you who the protagonists are and what the outcome is for each of them. By identifying what the outcome is and whom it belongs to help give you, the writer, a sense of direction in regards to where you are going with your story. This sense of direction is what you want to keep in mind during the entire writing process as all events, thoughts, conversations, and other actions should ultimately lead up to it.

Step Three: Turning Your Idea into a Story

Once you have an idea and a sense of direction, it is time to turn your idea into a story. A great way to work with this part of the process is to start with the very basics and then build from there. That being said, start by writing down what you already know about your story. Anything you have already planned, brainstorm it on a piece of paper. Next, turn this brainstorm into some basic plot points. Be sure to add some twists, turns, unexpected events, wins, and losses along the way. Then, when you have completed that, take another piece of paper and write these points out along a plot line. If you are using lined paper, leave a few lines between each point. Don't worry about how you are going to organize these onto the story arc, they don't need to be in chronological form just yet. Instead, focus on getting them written down. Once you have, then you can start elaborating on the details of each of these points. Consider how each plot point contributes to the greater story and what should be involved so that it can contribute in a strong way. The best way to look at it is to view these unique plot points as tools. Each one will be used to drive your story forward and tell a certain part of it. You want to ensure that these tools are equipped with all of the pieces that they will need to provide a strong driving factor for your story. You don't necessarily need to know all of the factors of the story, but you should be taking the time to learn as much as possible. Ideally, you want to have at least 4-6 sentences about each plot point where you identify as many details about that plot point as you can. Remember, they don't need to be in chronological order so simply make sure that you are writing down anything that comes to mind that would be important to the story itself. As you are writing, you may find that you are in need of additional plot points so be sure that you take the time to brainstorm these and elaborate on them as well. This will ensure that you have all of the substance you need to generate a strong plot for your story.

Step Four: Create Your Story Arc

Now, you want to begin creating your story arc. This is going to be the outline that was described in chapter one, with the exposition, rising action, climax, falling action, and resolution. You can write this in list form by identifying each element of the arc, or you can draw it out on a piece of paper so that you can plan out your plot as though you are creating a timeline for your novel. Each method works, and in fact, it may be beneficial for you to do both, starting with the list and then moving over to the diagram, if you feel that you do better with the opportunity to both plan it out on a list and then get an idea of the final effect on the diagram.

Creating your story arc this way is what will ultimately give you the opportunity to get an idea of how your story looks overall. For this part, you want to step back from your detailing and look at the greater picture. Here is where you are going to identify where each plot point fits on the diagram, and where it should be placed in relevance to the other events taking place. Before you get started with placing anything on your diagram, read steps six and seven as they will provide you with important information about how you can do this effectively.

Step Six: Start with The End

When it comes to creating your plot, you want to start with the end. Remember, this is the direction you are heading in, and this is where you want your story to end up. You should be able to get an idea of what your end is going to look like based on the focus sentence you generated in step two. Now, however, you want to elaborate on that. This is going to be the first official plot point you outline on your story arc. Fortunately, it is an easy one. This point lies at the end of the map, so you can place it at the very end of your story arc. Once you have, identify what needs to happen in order for you to know that the end has been reached. What that means is identify the conditions, the state of mind, and any other relevant information that will take place at the end of the book that will be an indicating factor to you that the story has matured and is now ready to be ended.

As you read in step five, it is not necessary for you to go into specific detail about this point altogether as this should have already happened in step three when you were describing and elaborating on each plot point. Instead, simply refer back to that brainstorm if you need more information about all of the details surrounding the ending of your story.

Step Seven: Organize Your Plot Points on the Story Arc

Once you have identified the end-point, you want to start organizing the remaining plot points along your story arc. Now, this is the part where you need to pay attention. Here is where you may choose to put less detail into it if you want, especially if there are certain elements that you simply don't know yet, but ultimately having this plan created in the way that we are about to explore is what will ensure that you are clear on the focus and direction of your book and what you need to do to arrive at the outcome.

You want to start by working backward along the plot points. Pay attention to what your end point is, and then write everything on the line going backward from there. Reverse engineering your plotline in this way will ensure that you cover all of the important plot factors and that everything happens chronologically *for* your outcome, rather than it randomly appearing out of nowhere. Doing this actively ensures that everything makes sense and that it is built in the most solid form possible. It also ensures that your plot contains all of the information that is needed, and that you can easily find where each plot point belongs based on what needs to happen *before* the last plot point in order for it to have even occurred in the first place. For example, in order for the bank robber to rob the bank, he must first plan the robbery, therefore placing the plan *before* the action. Use this frame of thinking for each of your plot points, and they will all fall together on the line effortlessly.

Step Eight: Tying it All Together

Once you have successfully identified all of the different plot points, step back and take a look at your overall story arc. Pay attention to the different points you have included, and where everything falls. If it is too crowded, you may consider eliminating some of the less important plot points from the story arc so that you are not going further than what actually is required for the story itself. Alternatively, if you notice anything is missing take this time to identify what it is and include it in your story arc. Once you have, review it one more time to make sure all of the elements fit on it well and that they are all contributing to the overall story itself.

Finally, the best way to bring it all together is to write a few sentences about your story arc. Essentially you want to give an overview of your story based strictly on each plot point you have added on the story arc. For example, "Angela is a barista who has been working for a local coffee shop for six years. She recently met a new friend, Sam, who has been getting her into a lot of trouble. Her boss was worried about her, but this only made Angela feel guilty. To avoid the guilt, she quit her job as a barista and pursued a job in a sketchy nightclub with Sam. This lead to the girls being taken advantage of by a patron of the club, which ultimately leads them to find themselves in a basement of an unknown building." You would carry on writing sentences that walk you through each plotline along the way as this helps you see the flow of how your story will go. Obviously, you want to go into much more detail when writing the story and actually bring the reader along with you. However, writing it in this way allows you to see everything and make sure it all works together well. It can also help you identify anywhere that your plot may need to be altered, reorganized, strengthened, or otherwise adjusted to benefit the overall story.

It is vital that you take the time to look over the entire plotline after it has been laid out because this is what will ensure that you have made the best one possible. Of course, your plotline doesn't need to be intensely elaborate and overdone, but having it clearly defined and knowing the important details of each plot point will ensure that you have plenty to write about. It also helps ensure that you are clear on the direction of your story and that you don't end up going off track somewhere during the writing process. Furthermore, if you find that you are feeling stuck from an episode of writer's block, you can consult your plot line to help you move forward and stay on track with your writing.

Creating your plotline can take anywhere from a few hours to a few days. It all depends on how much time you are willing to invest in the process and how much you already know, or don't know, about your story. For some people, getting the inspiration for the story itself can take a few days or even weeks. Don't be discouraged if you find that this isn't a quick one-afternoon job for you. The best stories take time to accumulate, and they are well-planned in advance. The more prepared you are now, the stronger your story will be in the long run. While you don't need to plan so deeply that you take away any opportunity for you to be creative during the writing process, it certainly benefits to have clarity around your book, your goals, and what you envision the end result to be with your story.

Chapter 3: Bringing Your Plot to Life

Bringing your plot to life happens entirely through the writing process. However, there are many ways that you can ensure that you activate the right techniques during this process to really bring your plot to life. Ultimately, bringing your plot to life is the process of taking your story from being an outline on a page to being an actual book that moves your readers and keeps them engaged and invested in your book all the way until the end. In this chapter, we are going to identify important tips to consider when it comes to writing around your plot to ensure that it comes to life effectively for your reader.

Consider How Your Characters Fit In

Your characters are the voice to your story. They are also the tools you use to move your story from point to point. This makes them an extremely important element of your story overall. You will learn more about in-depth character development in the book "Character Development" of this series, but in the meantime, you should consider how they fit in overall. This is the part where you want to consider how each character is going to fit into the plot points, as well as how they will be affected by them. Primarily, you want to think about how each point will affect your protagonist and your antagonist. The more you are aware of how they are being affected, the easier it will be for you to write a compelling story that has your readers genuinely believing each point.

Since you haven't already established the in-depth portion of your characters, you should consider them in a general sense. For example, "In chapter six, Elise moves away which causes Jonathan to feel lost. Elise is affected by this move because she is moving away from her best friend and into a place where she doesn't know anyone. Jonathan is affected because he has a crush on Elise but he never managed to say anything before she left and now he doesn't think he will ever get the opportunity to tell her how she truly feels. He knows pursuing her dream career is good for her, but he can't help but feel a sense of guilt and hopelessness around the entire situation."

It is important that you consider your characters in each situation because this will help you get inside of their head more. This is important for character development, which you will learn about, but it is also important for story development. You want to make sure that the events move forward in a way that flows and is natural for the characters within' your story. If you are unsure about how to consider your characters in various plot points, use this generic question: "How does x affect y because of z?" For example, "How does moving affect Jonathan because of his love for Elise?" This question will help get you thinking about how each part of the book affects your characters and then plan out how you can use this in both the planning and writing processes.

Hide the Plot Effectively

When you are writing a plot, it is important that you learn to hide the plot effectively. Even though most readers are aware that there is a climax that typically involves some form of large conflict in virtually every book, it doesn't mean that they want to see the points of the plot sloppily put into every part of the book. Instead, they want to read the book and have that as a natural flow that is hidden in the background. Seamlessly hiding the plot within' your book requires a fair amount of practice, as well as a few techniques. One you will learn in the next section, which involves effectively transitioning between plot points. Another includes giving enough detail to each plot point within' the book that it is well discussed and does not feel as though it has been rushed through. Rushing through plot points detracts from the quality of your book and takes away from the reader experience by not giving them enough information about each plot point. You want to make sure that your reader understands why each element of the story exists and how it ultimately contributes to the story itself. It should feel as though the flow is moving naturally, not slow and not rushed.

Hiding the plot sequencing and story arc within' your story effectively means that your reader should not be able to easily identify when the next major story plot is coming, or what it will be. If you are not using a dynamic plot line and hiding it effectively, there is a good chance that your reader will be able to identify what your story is and determine the major plot points and outcome well before they ever got to those parts of the story. This takes away from the reading experience and generally leads to them putting the book down and not finishing it because they simply can't stay engaged. Effectively building and hiding your plotline avoids this.

Effective Transitioning Between Plot Points

It is important that you learn to effectively transition between plot points. If you are not highly practiced with this, you may want to identify what will take place during the transitions *before* you begin writing. These transition phases are heavily important to the story overall because they contribute to the natural flow of the story. Think about it, your life is not a series of major events. There are several things that take place in between the major things that happen in your life. The day-to-day events. While you don't want to bore your readers by repetitively sharing the same day over and over throughout the story, you also want to make sure that you give insight to your character's daily lives and what the calm is like between the storm. Take the time to naturally transition the plot along the major points, rather than simply jumping from one to the next. This is what gives your story a natural flow and prevents it from sounding stiff or uncomfortable.

There are many ways that you can transition between different plot elements, several of which will arise naturally as you are writing. However, the following points will give you some ideas as to how you can transition points if you are feeling stuck.

- Talk about day-to-day life, but switch it up with each transition that you use this strategy for. You may refer back to certain points, but don't explain the exact same events in great detail over and over. Instead, highlight different elements of the day-to-day experiences in between each transition.

- End the chapter and start the next one. While you don't want to use this strategy every time, it is a great way to start suspense. Make sure you don't jump right into the climax of the next plot point with the new chapter, but rather that you build up to it from a new angle than you would have with where you were previously. This also helps build suspense.

- Talk about the falling action from the previous plot point and then transition into the rising action of the next plot point.

You want to change up which strategy you use each time you are conducting a transition as using the same ones frequently can result in the book becoming predictable. While new chapters should bring new plot points, for example, they shouldn't happen at exactly the same time with the new chapter. You should not immediately feast into the rising action and place the climax of the new plot point within' the first page or two of the chapter. Instead, let the rising action linger, or even blend together two unique transition strategies for greater impact. The more you vary your approach and use unique angles, the better your overall story will be.

Have Action-Packed Plot Points

Plot points are meant to move the story forward, and while not all of them will be action-packed, you should certainly have a fair bit that it. Action-packed plot points encourage the reader to become further engaged in your book. They become interested in what is happening, how it ties into what has already happened, and what it could mean for the characters going forward. Effectively action-packed plot points littered throughout your story keeps it active and engaging for your readers, and it also helps move you forward toward the outcome. Action is where the motion is, so you want to use this tool as a strategy to help you move the story forward.

When you are using action-packed plot points, make sure you don't go too overboard. First, you want to have some of your plot points that are built differently, such as around emotional points. This will ensure that your reader doesn't become overwhelmed with action. Second, you want to make sure that the action makes sense to the story, that it moves the story forward, and that it doesn't overwhelm the reader. Using too much action can result in your reader feeling overwhelmed and struggling to keep up with your story. It also leads to them feeling disconnected from the story because they simply cannot relate to it; it doesn't seem like a realistic situation that would ever happen and therefore they are pulled out of the story.

Using action-packed plot points is a great tool that does not need to be used sparingly, but it does need to be used effectively. If you are interested in how you can add these to your story, consider looking at your overall plot and seeing where the action-based plot points are. Pay attention to what the action is, how it affects the story, and how you might be able to infuse more action into each plot point to get the most of it. However, make sure you keep a few that feature action but still have a more profound sense to them. These are the ones where something major happens, but it's not necessarily built around "and then, and then, and then." Instead, there is a large event that takes place which isn't clouded by several other events. This is a great way to make an event more profound, so if you need a certain plot point to carry a lot of meaning, make this one of the ones where there is less action built into it and more emotion built into it instead.

Make the Plot Engage the Reader's Emotions

In addition to having a plot that uses action to drive the story forward, have a plot that activates various emotions within' the reader to keep them engaged. Emotional attachment is what encourages a reader to stay connected to the story. When they develop a sense of attachment and concern for the protagonist, as well as some form of emotional resentment against the antagonist, readers are more likely to stay engaged in the book. Because they are genuinely invested in knowing how things turn out for the characters within' the book, they are more compelled to keep reading.

You can engage the reader's emotions in a variety of ways, but ultimately how you do so will be a part of your plot building. This is also a large part of what brings the plot to life for people. If they do not have a reason to care, they simply won't care. Instead, they will tune out. When you give people a reason to care, however, they are more interested, and therefore the entire story comes to life and fuels a passion within' them to carry forward. They feel empathy for your characters, and therefore you have the power to engage other emotions within' them to further draw them in and keep them moving forward.

The best way to engage emotions is to use the characters at each plot point to do so. For example, if someone dies in one of the plot points you can use the reactions of the characters to spark emotions such as relief, grief, anger, or otherwise. How you choose to spark emotions heavily relies on your decision, as well as where you want the story to go. This is all about the outcome, remember. You should seek to activate several of your reader's emotions throughout the duration of the story. While you don't want to infuse too many emotions into each situation, the story as a whole should dance on the emotional heartstrings of your readers in many different ways. The more emotional the experience is, the more enjoyable the read is.

Once again, you want to make sure that you are using emotions within' reason. You shouldn't be attempting to forcefully push your readers into extreme states of any given emotion. Instead, you want to suggest emotions through the actions, reactions, words, and thoughts of your characters and allow your reader to take it the extra mile on their own. Pushing it too hard can make it feel forced and unnatural, therefore taking away from the reading experience itself. You want the emotion to be believable, natural, and aligned with the story you are telling in each given moment throughout the book. When it comes to generating emotional reactions from your readers, you want to look at the book as a whole. See how you can use emotions overall, rather than how you can use them in each given moment. This will help you move your reader through emotions in a natural, well-developed way.

When it comes to infusing emotions, there is typically a certain way that emotions are infused into a plot line. In the beginning, readers are given opportunities to develop emotional attachments to the characters, so you want to emphasize on empathy in this part of the book. When you build empathy effectively here, you give your readers a reason to care for the rest of the book.

Next, you want to play on that empathy to generate a healthy connection between the characters and your reader as you are building the rising action in your plot line. Here, you want to use a lot of positive and happy emotions. You also want to use some feelings of sadness, grief, anxiety, anger, fear, and other emotions to help build up a sense of what the stakes mean for your character. These emotions also help build suspense and get your reader emotionally invested in the conflicts that are happening to your characters.

At the climax, you want to have a lot of energy built up. The specific emotion you emphasize on will depend on your unique genre. It may be love, anger, relief, resentment, frustration, fear, anxiety, or any other number of emotions depending on your genre and the story you are telling. This emotion is the one you want to charge the most as it is the highest point of your story. Therefore your reader really needs to *feel* like it is while they are reading.

As you move through the falling action, you want to highlight emotions like empathy, grief, sorrow, relief, and other emotions that you would typically feel after something major has finally happened. Again, the exact emotions you will use will be unique to your unique story. There are also a few important emotions you want to infuse into this part of your story. This part of your story should particularly focus on hope, faith, forgiveness, and rebuilding and moving forward with their lives. Since this is the path towards the resolution, you want them to genuinely feel that the resolution is coming and that the character feels hopeful for it, too. While they may lose hope sometimes, it should be a lingering emotion in the background.

When the novel ends, you typically want to give the reader a sense of closure. This is where you can give them the "happily ever after" that most readers come for. This could be a happily ever after where the characters truly achieved happier lives, or it could be one where they live the happiest version of their life that they possibly can based on the traumatic experiences that the characters recently endured. Once again, this will heavily depend on your story and the genre you are writing in. For example, romantic novels typically end in a feel-good happily ever after where the two lovers end up together and lead charmingly romantic lives until their old age. Alternatively, a mystery novel where someone is murdered in the beginning and the duration of the novel is spent discovering who did it should have a happily ever after whereby the murderer is found, the case is solved, justice is served, and the characters can move on with their healing process.

Chapter 4: Best Plot Building Advice

The basic plot-building advice and the eight-step process in chapter 2 give you a great foundation for creating your plot outline. However, you want to make sure that you take it that extra step further and have a great plot outline, and not just a "done" one. The following advice will help give you an insight as to how you can strengthen your plot and create a powerful one that will drive your story forward. These tips and tricks are provided from some of the best writers themselves, so you can trust that they are sound and will help you with building and troubleshooting your own plot!

Never Skip the Plot Building Process

The first tip you should know is that you never want to skip the plot building process. Even if you already know most of the information you want to share in your mind, you still want to build the plot. Building a plot allows you to get the information out of your mind and take it from a great plot to a phenomenal one. This process enables you to go deeper, question yourself and your intentions, and increase the quality of the plot overall. It also ensures that you can organize it and stay focused so that your story remains on track. It truly is essential in generating a well-structured, chronological and focused plot line that will drive your story forward and keep readers engaged.

Failing to create a plot line is truly a tragedy when it comes to your results. It often leads to the story lacking the depth that it could have, and ultimately not reaching its full potential. Because you didn't allow yourself to further explore your purpose, your plan, and your direction, you were never able to elaborate on it and strengthen it in a way that would serve your story even more than your initial idea already did. It can also lead to your story being sloppy, disorganized, and all over the place in such a way that your readers simply cannot follow, and therefore they fail to become engaged and stay invested in reading your book. If you want to have a book that makes sense, that engages your readers, and that has them craving more of your work, then you absolutely must start with a plot outline.

Build Strong Characters to Compliment Your Plot

Your plot is only as strong as your characters are. If you build a strong plot but fail to generate the right characters that can be used to drive the plot forward, you are not going to have a great story. Having a strong story that your readers will love ultimately comes from focusing on all elements of the story, including the plot. You should not primarily focus on the plot, the characters, the structure, or any other element of the story. Instead, you want to make sure that each individual part is well-developed so that they all work together like a well-oiled machine. Not only does this make the writing process easier, but it also maximizes the quality of your book and ensures that it reaches its fullest potential in all aspects.

Your characters are the ones that are involved in the plot, and they are the ones that you are speaking and acting through to drive it forward. If they are not developed enough, are not created specifically for the plot, or otherwise struggle to carry your plot forward, you are not going to have an incredible story. In fact, you may not even have a great one. Instead, you may have a mediocre one that was lost on characters who were not strong enough to carry the story forward. In the next book, you will learn about how you can develop your own characters, and you will also be walked through an in-depth character building exercise that allows you to generate the best possible characters. Ensure that you take the time to use that and build characters specifically for your story and plotline so that they carry it forward and lead you towards complete success with your book.

Have a Powerful Outcome

The outcome of your story is what it's all about. Literally, the entire story building up to that point is only there for that specific point. People want to know how things turn out for all of the characters involved so they remain invested until the end, curious about what the outcome will be. If your outcome is not powerful enough, your readers are going to be heavily disappointed. There are a few things to keep in mind when it comes to developing your outcome, which we will explore now.

First, you want to avoid your outcome being too "flat" for the story. It should be full of some form of emotion that leaves your reader genuinely feeling something when the book ends.

119

They should feel hopeful, grateful, happy, or otherwise positive about the ending of the story. Additionally, they should feel as though they have been granted with closure from the ending. Your reader should feel that all loose ends have been tied and that anything that was lingering in the story was explained before you drew the story to a close. They should be feeling satisfied and complete with the story you have provided, and not like they are left wondering about any other element. Unless, of course, you are purposefully ending on a cliffhanger to help draw them into the next book of a series, you want to avoid leaving your readers with a cliffhanger. Instead, you want to provide them with a sound ending that makes them feel happy for the character like their goal was achieved because they accomplished what they had set out to accomplish in the beginning when we were presented with the primary problem.

When you are generating your outcome, you also want to make sure that it leaves a powerful impact on your reader. This comes from the emotions, but it should come from the thoughts as well. A great way to do this is to leave them reflecting on a part of their own life, reflecting on the story itself, or even feeling as though they have learned a lesson through the reading process. The ending should be sort of like a grand finale for your reader, complete with a drum roll and fireworks.

Use a Natural Ending Point

To elaborate on how to end your story, you want to ensure that you choose a natural ending point. You do not want to pick a spot that feels unnatural like something has been left unsaid, or like the reader isn't getting the full gist of the story. You also don't want to carry on well after the natural ending point has come as this will dilute the quality of your ending. Instead, you want to make sure that you keep it powerful by providing plenty of information, but only the necessary information. It is important that you remember that the outcome is the part of the book that will remain freshest in your readers mind so this is the part that should have the biggest impact on them.

Let Your Characters Resolve Their Own Conflict

Many stories fall flat when they let a force of nature or some unknown hero come in and save their characters from the problems that have arisen throughout the story. In some cases, this helps. In the majority, however, it is a very weak technique that takes away from the story. Readers are drawn into a story because they develop a connection to the character. So, naturally, they want to watch the character develop and see the natural conflict resolution by the character. They want to know how this has changed them, how it has helped them grow, and what they have learned from it. Not only does this allow the reader to feel as though they are spying through a peephole into the life of the character, but when done properly it also helps the reader learn some things from the character, too. When readers feel connected to the character, it is often because they relate in some way. Therefore, when the character naturally evolves, it causes the reader to look within' themselves and see how they have grown, or how they might grow in the future as a result of what they have witnessed in your characters. For this to happen, however, there has to be a change in your character that takes place naturally. This means that it is important that you let your character resolve their own conflict. While you can allow heroes and random acts of nature take the credit on smaller subplots within' the story, it is important that the major changes and lessons are directly through the character themselves.

Be Original

If the story you are writing has already been written and you are only changing the names and a few basic points in the book, you are going to lose traction with readers. Books that are outstanding and that become known as great and even phenomenal books are ones that are written out of originality. Everything else gets tossed in the bargain bin within' a few days from their launch. You want to make sure that you are writing an original story that your reader will not feel like they have already read. If they feel like the story is too similar to another one they have read, then your story becomes both predictable and unexciting. You may even damage your writing reputation by essentially copying someone else's work. And, if you're not careful, you could infringe on plagiarism rules. It is important that you generate an original plot that your reader doesn't know from previous stories. While it will certainly share similarities to others in the genre and it may borrow some ideas or techniques from other books, the overall product should be unique and original from what has already been written and released. This will ensure that you keep your readers engaged and interested throughout the reading process and that your story has the potential to climb to best-seller rating, rather than simply be skimmed through and dropped just as quickly.

Use an Exciting Plot

Readers don't *want* to get engaged with your book, they *need* to. If you use a plot that lacks excitement, you are going to struggle to get your readers engaged, and therefore you will fail to meet their expectations and have them raving about your book. Instead, they will simply close the book and won't recommend it to anyone else. Or, worse, they will leave a negative review on reviewing platforms about your book, discouraging others from giving it a chance, too. What you need is an exciting plot that will keep your readers engaged and invested from the time they open the book until the time they finish reading it. Your readers should feel like they don't want to put the book down when they're reading it, and like they can't wait to get back to it once they have. They should be heavily invested in the characters, the stakes, the conflicts, and the story itself. Doing this requires you to have an exciting plot.

An exciting plot is one that moves forward. It should not go straight from point A to point B, though. Instead, it should take many unexpected twists, turns, and side steps as it advances towards the final outcome. The reader should not know what to expect, but they should be emotionally invested in each part of it. Every plot point that you include should contribute to the overall story in some way, even if the reader doesn't understand how right away, or until much later. The more effectively you keep the story exciting and interesting, the more you will generate raving readers who are eager to share your book with others and encourage them to give it a read themselves.

Switch Up the Pace

When it comes to writing a fiction novel, you always want to emphasize on how it compares to reality. Even if you are writing a fantasy novel, the pace at which the book moves should be comparable to reality itself. There should be parts where it is fast, and parts where it moves slower. There should be areas where strong emotions are sparked, and there should be areas where no emotions are sparked. Your reader should feel as though the book ebbs and flows, much like an ocean tide. This gives them the opportunity to move along with the story at a natural, realistic pace. During the times of action and emotion they are heavily engaged and are rapidly being fed new information, and during the times of calm and more relaxing emotions, they are given the opportunity to reflect on recent events while also seeing how the characters are doing the same. Switching up the pace gives your book a realistic flow that keeps readers believing it to be true and maintains their ability to relate to it in some way at most times.

Stay On Track

Subplots are a great way to add depth to your book. However, too many can result in your book going off track and becoming confusing to the reader. You should not be darting around with information, sharing too many subplots, or diving into information that is entirely irrelevant to the overall story. Instead, you want to make sure that you are staying focused on the end result. Any subplot that somehow contributes to the overall story by giving it depth, allowing you to further explain certain elements of people or the plot, or otherwise increasing the quality of your story should be considered. Those that add enough value that makes them worthwhile should be kept. All other subplots should be ignored. When it comes to staying focused, make sure that you never divulge into information that is entirely irrelevant to the story. Unless it is drawing the reader towards the outcome, teaching them more about your characters, or otherwise providing them with a value that contributes to the story itself, you should not be sharing it. Getting carried away with irrelevant information results in your reader becoming confused. It dilutes your story and makes your readers want to close the book because they simply don't grasp what you're trying to tell them.

Have A Strong "Why"

Your "why" is your outcome. It is the reason why you are writing the story. Are you writing it to teach people who murdered the person in the beginning? Are you writing it to share a romantic love story between two people? Are you doing it to dive deeper into a fantasy world that you have built in your imagination and to bring life to it? Are you doing it to teach your reader a lesson? Why are you writing your book? Knowing why the book is being written in the first place can help with a significant number of writing elements. Your why is ultimately what will help you generate your plot as it will ensure that you are creating plot points that are relevant to the overall story, or the "why." It also ensures that your story stays focused. Furthermore, it helps your readers feel the significance of your novel. Your "why" for writing it will also be their "why" for reading it. They need to feel the significance and impact of this so that they feel compelled to read your book in the first place and to continue reading it until it ends. This is how they will get the biggest impact from your book, so you want to make sure that you are clear as to why you are writing it in the first place.

Don't Abuse Writing Techniques

Writing techniques are like tools that you use to structure your story, create certain causes and effects, and ultimately design your entire story in a way that impacts the reader the way the story is intended to. They are an incredible selection of tools that you absolutely need to use to generate a phenomenal story that your readers will love. However, you have to be aware when using these techniques. You never want to abuse them by overusing them, using them in the wrong area, or otherwise misusing them. When they are not used properly, these techniques take away from the story, and you dilute their impact overall. It is important that you use the right techniques in the right places and that you don't overuse them so as to eliminate the effect they have on your story.

Learn as You Go

One of the best pieces of advice that can be given is to learn as you go. Don't be afraid to make mistakes, take on criticism, and increase your skill by actively practicing it. Remember, you can't learn something if you don't practice in the first place. You don't try something and become an overnight master with it. You have to use the skill, practice the skill, and expand on the skill as regularly as possible if you are going to become a master at it. The best writers got to where they are today by practicing, listening to feedback, and improving their own skills. One great way to go about it is to keep a notebook and write down feedback

129

you get, as well as ideas or thoughts you have along the way. This gives you something solid to look back on and reflect on when it comes to increasing your skill and doing better in the future.

Conclusion

Thank you for reading *"Plot Writing: Step-by-Step | Essential Story Plotting, Conflict Writing and Plotline Tricks Any Writer Can Learn"*. This book was designed to help you take your plot deeper, increase your writing skills, and give your story a greater sense of purpose to keep your reader engaged and entertained along the way.

I hope this book was able to provide you with new, revolutionary, and insightful tips and tricks to help you with your plot. I also hope that you were able to use the eight-step plot building guide to help you generate a plot that will powerfully drive your story so that you can create the next best-seller. Remember, these tips are ones that can take you to the next level, but it is up to you to implement and practice them if you are going to take it all the way. Only you have the power to materialize the stories in your head and share them with the world! Practicing will help you do this with maximum impact.

The next step is to create your own plot line that will enrich your story and carry it to the end. Remember, reverse engineering is the best way to ensure that your story features everything it requires, so always look at things backward, if not starting backwards to begin with. Additionally, make sure that you take the time to read the next book where you will learn to develop incredible characters that will compliment your plot perfectly and help you take your book to the top. Recall that a book is like a well-oiled machine whereby all of the elements such as the structure, plot line, outline, and characters are built together to operate seamlessly and create a relatable, realistic story that your readers will love. Each element should be individually developed with the intention of it being a part of the greater story so that they contribute to the greatness of your novel.

Thank you, and good luck!